The Challenger 1986:

A space shuttle explodes after lift-off

LIZ GOGERLY

Raintree

First published in Great Britain by Raintree,
Halley Court, Jordan Hill, Oxford OX2 8EJ, part of
Harcourt Education.
Raintree is a registered trademark of Harcourt
Education Ltd.

© Harcourt Education Ltd 2006
First published in paperback in 2007
The moral right of the proprietor has been
asserted.

Editorial: Andrew Farrow and Richard Woodham
Design: Victoria Bevan and AMR Design Ltd
Illustrations: David Woodroffe
Picture Research: Maria Joannou and
  Ginny Stroud-Lewis
Production: Chloe Bloom

Originated by Modern Age
Printed and bound in China by South China
  Printing Company

13 digit ISBN 978 1 4062 0287 8 (hardback)
10 09 08 07 06
10 9 8 7 6 5 4 3 2 1

13 digit ISBN 978 1 4062 0297 7 (paperback)
11 10 09 08 07
10 9 8 7 6 5 4 3 2 1

British Library Cataloguing in Publication Data
Gogerly, Liz
The Challenger, 1986. - (When disaster struck)
363.1'24'16'09759
A full catalogue record for this book is available
from the British Library.

Acknowledgements
The publishers would like to thank the following
for permission to reproduce photographs:
Alamy p.18 (Ian Dagnall/NASA); Corbis pp.8
(Bettmann), 14, 15, 16-17, 19, 22, 24), 25
(Bettmann), 28 (Bettmann), 29 (Bettmann),
31, 34 (Bettmann), 39 (Bettmann), 41, 48
(Bettmann); Empics p.47; Getty Images
p.26 (Michael R.Brown/Liaison); John Frost
Newspapers p.33; NASA pp.4 (Kennedy Space
Center), 6 (Kennedy Space Center), 11 (Johnson
Space Center), 12 (Johnson Space Center), 13
(Johnson Space Center), 16 (Johnson Space
Center), 21 (Johnson Space Center), 36 (Johnson
Space Center), 38 (Johnson Space Center), 42
(Johnson Space Center), 44 (Johnson Space
Center), 45 (Kennedy Space Center), 46 (Johnson
Space Center), 49 (Johnson Space Center); Rex
Features p.35; Science Photo Library p.10 (NASA);
Topham Picturepoint p.27.

Cover photograph of *Challenger* reproduced with
permission of Corbis.

The publishers would like to thank Henry M.
Holden for his assistance in the preparation of
this book.

Every effort has been made to contact copyright
holders of any material reproduced in this book.
Any omissions will be rectified in subsequent
printings if notice is given to the publishers.

CONTENTS

Any words appearing in the text in bold, **like this**, are explained in the glossary.

Note: times quoted in the text are US Eastern Standard Time.

A SPACE SHUTTLE EXPLODES AFTER LIFT-OFF

The *Challenger* 1986

COUNTDOWN TO DISASTER

On 28 January 1986, at 11:38 a.m. EST, the space shuttle *Challenger* launched from Kennedy Space Center in Florida, United States.

It was a magnificent sight. The noise of the engines was deafening as fire and smoke burst out of them. People all over the world were watching the event on television. This was a special **mission** because the first **civilians** were going into **space**. Once the shuttle had cleared the launch pad, people began to relax.

Just over a minute later, there was a sudden burst of fire as *Challenger* exploded. Huge clouds of white smoke filled the sky above. It was 73 seconds after lift-off. *Challenger* and all 7 crew on board were lost in the explosion.

Challenger spiralled back down to Earth, trailing smoke.

A NEW ERA FOR SPACE FLIGHT

The *Challenger* 1986

THE FIRST PEOPLE IN SPACE

Challenger exploded about 25 years after the first human being flew into space.

In April 1961 Major Yuri Gagarin, from the **Soviet Union**, became the first man to travel in space. The following month, Alan Shepard became the first American **astronaut** in space. The following decades were an exciting time. The world watched increasingly daring missions live on television.

The cost of sending early spacecraft into space was very high. They could only be used once. One method of cutting back on costs was to design a reusable spacecraft. In the early 1970s, the National Aeronautics Space Administration (**NASA**) began working on a Space Transportation System (STS), also known as the space shuttle. In 1981 _Columbia_ became the first space shuttle to be launched. It was the beginning of a new **era** for space flight.

On 12 April 1981, _Columbia_ lifted off from Kennedy Space Center.

IS IT A ROCKET OR IS IT A PLANE?

The space shuttle has the power of a rocket but can be flown like an aeroplane. It can be used this way because it is made from three major parts. One part is called the **orbiter**. The orbiter looks like an aeroplane. On returning to Earth, the pilot lands it on a runway like an aeroplane. The shuttle also contains solid-fuel booster rockets. The booster rockets provide the enormous **thrust** that the shuttle needs at its launch. These rockets are **discarded** about two minutes after lift-off. They fall into the sea. The third part of the shuttle is the external fuel tank. The fuel tank holds the huge amount of liquid fuel needed for the shuttle to launch. The fuel tank is also discarded after about the first eight-and-a-half minutes of flight.

A poster from 1972 showed how the shuttle could be used in the future.

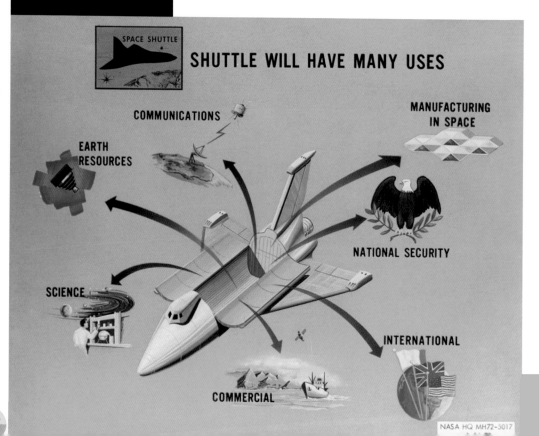

SPACE SHUTTLE

SHUTTLE WILL HAVE MANY USES

COMMUNICATIONS

MANUFACTURING IN SPACE

EARTH RESOURCES

NATIONAL SECURITY

SCIENCE

INTERNATIONAL

COMMERCIAL

NASA HQ MH72-5017

NASA believed that using the space shuttle would cost less than using rockets. This was because the orbiter can be reused. The orbiter contains much of the expensive equipment needed for space exploration. At the front of the orbiter are the **flight deck** and **crew quarters**. An air-locked room with two hatches connects the flight deck to the **payload** bay. The payload bay is used for transporting cargo and scientific instruments. It is also where the Spacelab is located. Here, experiments about space and space travel take place.

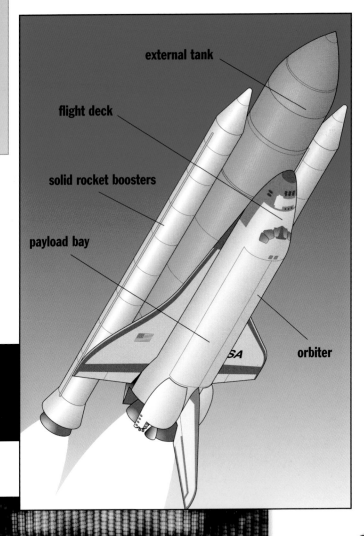

external tank

flight deck

solid rocket boosters

payload bay

orbiter

This diagram shows the different parts that make up the shuttle.

ALL SYSTEMS GO

Columbia, the first space shuttle, made its first journey into space on 12 April 1981. This was exactly 20 years to the day after Major Yuri Gagarin became the first man in space. *Columbia* stayed in space for two days. In that time it travelled over 1.6 million kilometers (1 million miles) and **orbited** the Earth 36 times. When it landed back on Earth, it was greeted with great excitement. The mission had gone well. Other than a few minor problems with the computer system, the shuttle had worked perfectly. Space travel had changed forever!

Challenger was the second space shuttle to fly into space. Lessons had already been learned about shuttle technology and *Challenger* had been upgraded from a test vehicle. It was built to last 10 years and make about 100 trips.

In 1983, *Challenger* successfully completed the first night launch and night landing.

Sally Ride, the first American woman in space, during training.

Challenger's first mission began on 4 April 1983. It was early days in shuttle technology. NASA was still planning missions for the shuttle to carry out. They were also finding out how space travel affected the astronauts. The **maiden voyage** of *Challenger* was particularly exciting because the crew completed the first spacewalk during a shuttle mission.

Just over two months later, *Challenger* was up in space again. This time the trip made history because one of the astronauts on board was Sally Ride, who became the first American woman in space. In August 1983 *Challenger* was in the news once again when Guion Bluford became the first African American in space. NASA had also successfully completed the first night launch and night landing.

REACTIONS TO THE SHUTTLE

"Gone were the great parachutes and swinging capsules of earlier space missions, splashing into the sea, never to travel into space again. For the first time, a man-made machine had returned from the heavens like an ordinary airplane – in fact, far more smoothly than many a commercial jet. So long delayed, so widely criticized, *Columbia's* flight should finally put to rest any doubts that there will one day be regular commuter runs into the cosmos."

TIME, April 1981

STEPPING INTO THE UNKNOWN

In February 1984 *Challenger*'s astronauts, Bruce McCandless II and Lieutenant Colonel Robert Stewart, made the first ever **untethered** spacewalk. This meant they had no **lifeline** holding them to the space shuttle. The only thing that kept them from floating off into space was a manned maneuvering unit (**MMU**). A MMU is like a jet-powered, flying chair. As McCandless made his first daring steps into space he said, "That may have been one small step for Neil, but it's a heck of a big leap for me." This was a play on the famous words of Neil Armstrong. When Armstrong became the first man to walk on the Moon in 1969 he said, "That's one small step for [a] man, one giant leap for mankind."

TIMELINE

CHALLENGER'S HISTORIC MISSIONS

Lift-off date	Historic moment
April 1983	First spacewalk to take place during a space shuttle mission
June 1983	Sally Ride becomes the first American woman in space
August 1983	Guion Bluford becomes the first African American in space
February 1984	First untethered spacewalk, by two American astronauts
October 1984	Kathryn D. Sullivan becomes the first American woman to make a spacewalk

Guion Bluford became the first African American in space in 1983.

The test drive of the MMU made exciting viewing on television. But this spacewalk was just a practice run for the more serious work to come. In April 1984 *Challenger* launched again. This time the mission was to repair a **satellite** called *Solar Max*. The US $150 million satellite had been out of action for 3 years. On day 3 of the mission, *Challenger* was pulled up to about 60 metres (200 feet) away from the satellite. Astronaut George Nelson then boarded the MMU. The plan was for him to guide the satellite to within reach of the shuttle's **remote-controlled** mechanical arm. The mechanical arm would then grab the satellite and bring it into the shuttle's cargo bay. Once there, the repair work could begin.

Astronauts made the first untethered spacewalk on 3 February 1984.

CARTWHEELS IN SPACE

The mission did not go as planned. It was a reminder that a lot can go wrong in space exploration. The satellite would not stay still and at one point was turning cartwheels. Nelson was also unable to nudge the satellite within reach of the mechanical arm. For 36 hours the crew of *Challenger* tried to bring the satellite on board. The mission seemed destined to fail. It took courage and determination to finally wrestle the satellite into the cargo bay. That was such a triumphant moment that even President Ronald Reagan rang the crew to congratulate them. "Terry, you made one long reach for man this morning," the President told mission specialist Terry Hart, the controller of the mechanical arm.

Repair work could now begin. Within a few days, the crew set *Solar Max* back in orbit. For the first time, a satellite had been repaired in space. As one of the crew put it, "the era of the throwaway satellite is over." A replacement satellite would have cost about US $200 million.

SPACELAB

Spacelab is the name of the laboratory on board each space shuttle. It is a special pressurized cabin where the astronauts can work. The astronauts can also experiment on themselves. For example, they find out what effect space travel has on their muscles and bones. They also find out how it affects their senses or energy levels. These experiments help scientists to plan for future missions.

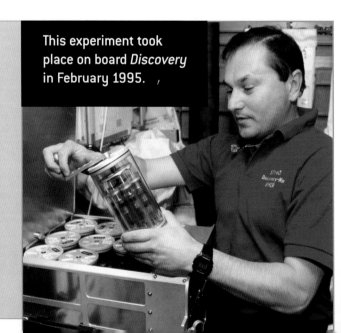

This experiment took place on board *Discovery* in February 1995.

Once in space the shuttle can become a **laboratory**. Many different scientific experiments can be carried out. When *Challenger* went on the mission to repair *Solar Max*, it also had 57 different experiments on board. These were placed in a special container called a long-duration exposure facility. This was left in space until the following February. Then *Challenger* returned to space and picked it up.

Many of the experiments used everyday objects. One experiment looked at how being in space affected the sprouting and growth of tomato seeds. Another experiment looked at what effect being in space had on plastic.

The astronauts chosen for shuttle missions spend many hours training in this Shuttle Mission Simulator (SMS).

MISSION
STS-51-L

The *Challenger* 1986

CAREFUL PLANNING

The astronauts selected for shuttle missions come from around the world.

They undergo basic training for a year. This includes being trained to deal with emergencies. Once the astronauts have finished the basics, they begin training for the role they will have on their mission.

By the end of 1985, *Challenger* had made nine trips. Each shuttle mission is given a special name. The tenth flight of *Challenger* was mission STS–51–L.

Mission STS–51–L was originally planned to take place on 1986 22 January, but the date was **postponed** because of delays to another shuttle mission. It was not until 1986 28 January that *Challenger* was ready for lift-off.

Challenger was carried on the back of a Boeing 747 to the launch site.

ANOTHER FIRST FOR CHALLENGER

In its short life, *Challenger* had already brought the world many firsts in space travel. The excitement surrounding the tenth mission was possibly the greatest yet. Children throughout America were excited because a teacher was going into space. *Challenger* was about to claim another first because that teacher was going to give a lesson while in orbit.

It had always been NASA's plan to take civilians into space. NASA believed that teachers and journalists would be good at telling other people about space exploration. In 1984 NASA announced its Teacher in Space Project (TISP). Over 10,000 teachers applied to be the first teacher in space. On 19 July 1985, NASA announced its choice. Thirty-six-year-old social studies teacher Christa McAuliffe, from New Hampshire, United States, was declared the winner.

▶ "THE ULTIMATE FIELD TRIP"

"It's the ultimate field trip [...] It's not often that a teacher is at a loss for words [...] I'm still kind of floating [...] I don't know when I'll come down to Earth."

Christa McAuliffe, on being chosen as the first teacher to go into space.

TIME, 29 July 1985

The NASA insignia (the "meatball") was designed in 1959.

Christa was planning to keep a diary while she was in space. More than anything, she wanted to make space technology interesting and easy for children to understand. She was also going to give two lessons while the shuttle was in orbit. These would be **transmitted** by satellite. The lessons were going to be called "The Ultimate Field Trip" and "Where We've Been, Where We're Going, and Why".

The other woman on board *Challenger* was Judith Resnik. She was an electrical engineer and was **appointed** a mission specialist. Judith was an experienced astronaut who had made her first shuttle trip on the *Discovery* in 1984. She once said, "I think something is only dangerous if you are not prepared for it or if you don't have control over it or if you can't think through how to get yourself out of a problem."

Christa McAuliffe spent months training for the *Challenger* mission.

THE CREW

"You know, it's a real crime to be paid for a job that I have so much fun doing." These words were spoken by Francis (Dick) R. Scobee, the commander of mission STS–51–L. In 1978 he was selected by NASA to train as an astronaut. By 1986 he had piloted a previous *Challenger* mission. When Dick Scobee climbed aboard the shuttle in January 1986, he had already spent 168 hours in space. He had also spent 6,500 hours flying 45 different types of aeroplane.

Dick Scobee was one of seven astronauts chosen for mission STS–51–L. Michael J. Smith was the pilot. He had begun training as an astronaut for NASA in 1980. He was proud to be part of the shuttle programme and believed it was extremely safe. The payload specialist was Gregory B. Jarvis. He was in charge of the experiments in the Spacelab. He had been selected by NASA for astronaut training in 1984 and this was his first shuttle mission.

TRAINING FOR WEIGHTLESSNESS

Each crew member must complete one year of basic training. This includes getting themselves ready for the weightlessness they will experience in space. In space there is no gravity to hold the body down. Astronauts float in all directions. To prepare for this strange feeling, the astronauts use a special chair. It is called a Five Degrees of Freedom machine. The chair allows them to move in any direction. Astronauts also practise in large water tanks.

Also on board were mission specialists Ronald E. McNair and Ellison S. Onizuka. McNair was the second African American in space. He had been selected by NASA in 1978 and had flown in *Challenger* before. He once said, "The true courage of space flight comes from enduring [...] perservering, and believing in oneself." He was a specialist in **deploying** satellites. Onizuka was the first Japanese American in space. He had joined NASA in 1978 and had spent 74 hours in space. It was his job to study the tail of **Halley's Comet**.

Front row, left to right: pilot Mike Smith, commander Dick Scobee, and mission specialist Ron McNair. Back row, left to right: mission specialist Ellison Onizuka, payload specialist and teacher Christa McAuliffe, payload specialist Greg Jarvis, and mission specialist Judy Resnik.

THE FINAL COUNTDOWN

The *Challenger* 1986

A COLD MORNING

Crowds of spectators shivered in the cold morning air as they waited to watch the launch of *Challenger*.

The morning of 28 January 1986 was one of the coldest days on record at Kennedy Space Center in Florida. The ice team had been called in to remove icicles from the launch pad. After that, everything was ready for lift-off. But the countdown stopped eight minutes before the shuttle was due to launch. There was a minor fault. This meant another delay for repair work.

The crew waited in the shuttle. Waiting probably gave them time to think about the tough job ahead of them. They may have thought about leaving their friends and family. All except Judith Resnik were married and most of them had children. However, they were professionals. They knew how to concentrate on doing their jobs. As Christa McAuliffe once said, "What are we doing here? We're reaching for the stars."

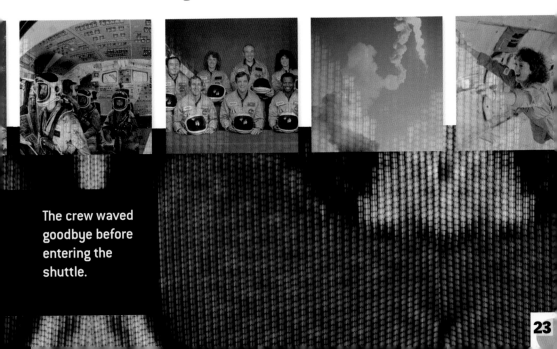

The crew waved goodbye before entering the shuttle.

THE GO-AHEAD

TIMELINE

T minus 1 minute:
Final safety checks complete. Crew harnessed into seats with their helmet visors down.

T minus 6 seconds:
The orbiter shudders as the main engines are fired.

T minus 5 seconds:
The orbiter leans forward as the engines build up power.

T minus 4 seconds:
Flames spit out of the rocket engines.

T minus 3 seconds:
The solid rocket boosters are lit.

T minus 1 second:
White flames and clouds of smoke pour out of the launch pad. The shuttle breaks free of the bolts holding it to the launch pad.

Lift-off:
The crew are thrust back into their seats as *Challenger* soars off the launch pad.

Four hours later the go-ahead was given for lift-off. The countdown began again. The crew prepared for launch again. There was still a chance that the launch could be aborted. In June 1984 Judith Resnik had been on the shuttle *Discovery* when the launch had been aborted just four seconds before lift-off.

Countdown was down to one minute. Safety checks were complete. Everything was now going smoothly. The crew checked that they were firmly strapped into their seats. Finally they put down their helmet visors. At last they were ready for lift-off.

The countdown continued. With six seconds to go, the main engines burst into life. Immediately the crew felt a huge surge of power. Below the craft three big rocket engines roared. "Three at 100," reported Dick Scobee, which meant that they had three fully working main engines.

The crew badge for mission STS–51–L included Halley's Comet, which the crew were planning to observe during the mission.

Challenger clears the launch pad on 28 January 1986. The ground shakes for miles around when a shuttle lifts off.

It was 11:38 a.m. and the crew were raring to go. The solid rocket boosters fired up. These provided the main thrust to lift the shuttle off the launch pad. Huge clouds of white smoke billowed into the cold morning air. Inside the shuttle the crew felt the thrust as the craft pushed off the launch pad. They were already travelling at 160 kilometres (100 miles) per hour when the launch tower fell away. "All riiiight!" cried Judy Resnik. "Here we go!" said Mike Smith.

▶ "THE LONGEST SIX SECONDS"

"[It's like] the longest six seconds of your life. The seconds count off while they check the engine and at that moment there is this huge kick in the pants, right in your back. Just everything starts. There is bone-jarring, shaking, and vibration. Your teeth are just chattering."

Andy Thomas, four times a crew member on a shuttle mission, describes his own experience of a shuttle launch.

THE EXPLOSION

It usually takes about 8 minutes and 30 seconds for the shuttle to reach space. It is then that the engines shut off and everything goes quiet. But the crew of *Challenger* never made it that far. They were still thrusting forward with all engines firing when things began to go wrong. Seventy-three seconds after lift-off, a white vapour appeared from the side of the craft. Milliseconds later there was an explosion. The final person heard on the cockpit voice recorder was the pilot, Mike Smith. "Uh-oh," were his last words.

The world's worth space disaster was witnessed by millions of Americans on live television. Many found it difficult to take in what they were seeing.

Spectators could not believe what they were seeing. Some shouted in disbelief. Other people just watched in silence. Their eyes were fixed on the once-perfect blue sky. Now it was filled with a great cloud of smoke. Trails of smoke came spiralling down like streamers. The trails of white smoke were pieces of wreckage falling into the sea.

In the blue skies above, *Challenger* broke up into pieces.

People watching the launch of *Challenger* on television saw the flames flaring out from the shuttle. At the White House the President's wife, Nancy Reagan, had been watching. "Oh, my God, no!" she cried. Back at Cape Canaveral, a space engineer pulled at his hair. "Where in hell is the bird? Where is the bird?" he yelled. The shuttle is often called the "white bird" by NASA workers.

SHOCK WAVES

The *Challenger* 1986

People at Kennedy Space Center watched in horror as *Challenger* exploded.

REALIZATION

At first there was shock and disbelief, before slowly everyone realized that it had really happened.

Among those watching at Cape Canaveral were Christa McAuliffe's parents. While everyone had cheered at lift-off, Christa's father had remained quiet. It was as if he had known something terrible was about to happen.

When it became clear there had been an accident, Christa's mother broke down in tears. Around them were children from the school where Christa taught. A few of them were already in tears. Others were asking when she would come back.

Some people in the crowd could not believe what they had seen.

"THEY SERVED US ALL"

President Ronald Reagan had been at the White House when he heard about the disaster. At 4:00 p.m. that afternoon he gave a speech live on television. His face was drained of colour and his eyes were heavy as he paid tribute to the crew of *Challenger*. "They had a hunger to explore the universe and discover its truths," he said. "They wished to serve, and they did – they served us all.'"

It was a moving speech and people were touched that the President remembered how children would be feeling on this terrible day. The Teacher in Space Project had been important for them. "I know it's hard to understand that sometimes painful things like this happen," President Reagan told them. "It's all part of the process of exploration and discovery, it's all part of taking a chance and expanding man's horizons."

At 4:30 p.m. on 28 January, NASA gave its first statement about the disaster. Jesse Moore, associate administrator for spaceflight at NASA, spoke of his "heartfelt sorrow". He claimed that nobody had seen anything unusual up until the point of the explosion. Then he told the public about the recovery ships that would comb an area of about 46 square kilometers (18 square miles) for wreckage. Helicopters and army planes would join in the search. NASA had also seized all the video footage and photographs of the disaster that had been taken by the major **news agencies**. People listening to Jesse Moore's speech wanted answers now but NASA was not going to say anything until it knew what had really happened.

THE REACTION FROM NASA

"I am aware and have seen the media showing footage of the launch today from the NASA select system. We will not speculate as to the specific cause of the explosion based on that footage. It will take all the data, careful review of that data, before we can draw any conclusions on this national tragedy."

Jesse Moore, associate administrator for spaceflight, NASA.

President Ronald Reagan appeared on television to express his regret at the accident. He read a moving poem called *High Flight*.

THE WORLD MOURNS

By the next day, the news had spread all over the world. Major leaders spoke of their sorrow and sympathy for the families of the astronauts. In Britain, Prime Minister Margaret Thatcher said, "New knowledge sometimes demands **sacrifices** of the bravest and the best. I just felt we saw the spirit of America and the spirit of the American people." In Italy, Pope John Paul II asked people to pray for the crew. Patrick Baudry, a French astronaut who had flown in the shuttle *Discovery* in 1985, offered some words of hope, "I think the sacrifice of my friends who were on board today will not be for nothing. There have been other accidents before. They have all served some purpose."

The story was on the front page of newspapers all around the world. "Spaceship Disaster – Teacher Dies Living The American Dream" was the headline in the *Daily Mail* in Britain. The *Sydney Daily Mirror* in Australia called it a "Space Horror". There was a terrible feeling of loss but already people were beginning to suggest reasons for the accident.

AMERICA MOURNS ITS SPACE HEROES

"The United States yesterday went into official mourning for the loss of the space shuttle *Challenger* and its crew of seven as the grim search for **debris** stretched over a 7,200 square-mile area of the Atlantic. Early speculation on the cause of the accident is focusing on the craft's large external fuel tank carrying some 385,000 gallons of liquid hydrogen and 140,000 gallons of oxygen at lift-off."

The *Guardian*, Thursday 30 January 1986

Daily Mail

WEDNESDAY, JANUARY 29, 1986   20p

MONEY MAIL TODAY

SPACESHIP DISASTER

Teacher dies living the American dream

Pioneer: Christa McAuliffe on way to the launch

IT was the moment that stunned the world: The American Space Shuttle Challenger explodes 75 seconds after lift-off, killing all seven astronauts on board. One of them was 37-year-old Christa McAuliffe, a schoolteacher from New Hampshire, chosen as the first 'ordin-ary citizen' to go into space. As America mourned, President Reagan, 'deeply concerned and shocked', postponed his annual State of the Union address, due last night. Instead, he broadcast to the nation on the disaster.

The horror — Pages 2, 3, 4 and 5

INSIDE: Weather 2, Lynda Lee-Potter 7, Femail 12, Diary 15, TV 26, 27, Casino Royale 30, Letters 32, Technology '86 34, 35, Sport 35-40

Newspaper headlines around the world expressed horror at the accident.

At the time of *Challenger's* launch there were about 500 journalists covering the story at the Kennedy Space Center. Another 30 were at the Johnson Space Center in Houston, Texas. Three days after the accident there were over 2,000 journalists and **broadcasters** in the area. There had not been so many journalists at one scene in the United States since the **assassination** of President Kennedy in 1963. The public desperately wanted to know what had happened. The journalists were eager to give them the latest news.

PIECING TOGETHER THE STORY

The first news came the day after the accident. NASA held another **press conference**. It announced that a **memorial service** for the crew would be held at the Johnson Space Center on 31 January. NASA also said it did not have enough evidence to say what had happened, but it had started to recover parts of *Challenger*. NASA had found parts of her wings and doors. At that point the bodies of the crew had not been found.

The US Coast Guard and the US Navy lifted parts of the shuttle from the Atlantic Ocean.

Teacher in Space

NASA

On Friday 31 January 1986, the memorial service went ahead. Before it began, President Reagan met with the close family of each of the crew. He hugged each one of them and picked up Mike Smith's eight-year-old daughter, Erin. Over 6,000 employees of NASA and 200 members of the astronauts' families gathered for the memorial service. Many people were in tears. Afterwards four T-38 jets flew overhead. T-38 planes are used during astronaut training. One of the jets moved sharply away from the other planes. This is called the "Missing Man Formation". It was used to symbolize the loss of the space shuttle *Challenger*.

▶ "WE WILL NEVER FORGET"

"The future is not free; the story of all human progress is one of a struggle against all odds. We learned again that this America [...] was built on heroism and noble sacrifice. It was built by men and women like our seven star voyagers, who answered a call beyond duty [...] Dick, Mike, Judy, El, Ron, Greg, and Christa – your families and your country mourn your passing. We bid you goodbye, we will never forget you."

President Ronald Reagan, speaking at the memorial service, 31 January 1986

WHAT
WENT
WRONG?

The *Challenger* 1986

A BILLION-DOLLAR DECISION

It would be months before people knew what really happened to *Challenger*.

And when they did find out, many people had serious doubts about NASA.

An hour after the explosion, NASA set up its own panel to discover what went wrong. On 3 February President Reagan set up a presidential commission to find out the truth. This was a panel of experts who had not been involved in the mission. Early findings suggested that NASA had not made safety a priority. The cold weather on the morning of 28 January should have been enough to postpone the launch. Now that the safety of the space shuttle programme was in question it had to be halted. The shuttle would be **grounded** for at least two years. NASA's decision to fly *Challenger* on that frosty January morning would ultimately cost it billions of dollars.

The shuttle was covered in icicles on the morning of the launch.

LOOKING FOR CLUES

Finding out what had happened to *Challenger* was an enormous job. There were hundreds of photographs and films of the launch to be examined. The designers and engineers who built the shuttle had to be interviewed. People involved in the launch had to be questioned, too. Large parts of the wreckage were taken back to Cape Canaveral. They were carefully inspected for clues.

Experts looking at film and photographs detected the first sign of a problem just 0.678 seconds after the launch. On a video tape, a puff of grey smoke could be seen coming from a joint on the right solid rocket booster. Moments later there were eight more puffs of smoke from the same joint. Next the experts saw a small flame appear on the rocket booster. *Challenger* had been on fire almost as soon as it launched.

The flame grew quickly and began spreading towards the external fuel tank. At 64 seconds after lift-off the flames reached the hydrogen fuel tank. Milliseconds later there was a bright glow on the underside of the shuttle. Then, 73 seconds into its flight, *Challenger* exploded.

Wreckage was examined at Complex 31 at Cape Canaveral Air Force Station.

In March 1986 the US Navy discovered the broken upper flight deck of *Challenger* about 29 kilometres (18 miles) east of Cape Canaveral. Inside, divers could see the bodies of some of the crew. They were still strapped into their seats. The divers said it was like finding a ghost ship.

Four **flight recorders** were also found. These gave more evidence about what had happened to *Challenger* and its crew. Some of the most awful questions about the final moments of the astronauts could finally be answered. The evidence suggested that the crew probably knew that they were in danger, but everything happened so quickly that they did not know for more than a couple of seconds.

A US Navy Honor Guard carries the coffin of pilot Michael Smith during his funeral service at the Fort Myer Post Chapel.

AN EXPERT'S OPINION

"It is likely that the crew was knocked unconscious immediately and felt nothing during the [three-to-four-minute] fall to the ocean. I want to guess that they were unconscious all the way down, if any of them really survived the fireball and breakup in flight."

Expert who examined the astronauts' bodies at Cape Canaveral, *TIME*, 24 March 1986

THE FAULTY O-RING

Eventually the presidential commission was able to find the reason for the accident. It had been caused by a fault in the joint between the two lower parts of the right solid rocket motor. The joints of the solid rocket motor are sealed with a loop of rubber-like plastic. The loop is called an O-ring seal. These seals were designed to prevent hot gases escaping through the joint when the rocket was burning. On this occasion the O-ring seals had failed. The gases had escaped and caught fire, eventually causing *Challenger* to explode.

Could the accident have been prevented? The presidential commission found plenty of evidence to suggest that people knew there were problems with the design of the O-rings. The manufacturer of the O-rings was a company called Morton-Thiakol. It had tested the O-rings in low temperatures and found that the O-rings became brittle in cold weather.

Two engineers from Morton-Thiakol had tried to stop NASA launching *Challenger* on that cold January morning, but NASA decided the fault in the O-rings was a "minor imperfection" and gave the all-clear for the launch. Was there a breakdown in communication at NASA? Should it have listened to the manufacturer's warning?

The report from the presidential commission was released on 9 June 1986. Though it criticized NASA, it also praised its achievements. The report laid down nine recommendations. These included reducing the number of launches each year. The report also suggested redesigning and testing the solid rocket motor. It also recommended new safety features to be added to the shuttle. These included introducing a new escape system with parachutes.

NASA IN TROUBLE

In 1986 NASA had other problems, too. On 18 April one of NASA's Titan rockets, carrying a Big Bird spy satellite, exploded. It was the second Titan rocket to explode within 12 months. Then, on 3 May, one of NASA's Delta rockets, carrying a satellite for spotting hurricanes, suffered engine failure. It had to be detonated. At that point the United States had no more spacecraft that could take satellites and other medium-sized payloads into space.

The problem that led to the explosion began in the right solid rocket booster, shown here.

CHALLENGER AND BEYOND

The Challenger 1986

NO MORE RISKS

After the *Challenger* disaster, NASA's new policy became "safety over schedule".

Another space shuttle mission did not take place for more than two years. In that time NASA redesigned parts of the shuttle. It also changed safety procedures. The next shuttle launch was postponed many times. NASA was often criticized for being too cautious, but nobody wanted to risk another disaster.

Without its space shuttle programme, the United States were unable to put satellites into space. The European Space Agency and China could do this using unmanned rockets. They could also do it for a lot less money. In 1986 the Soviets began building a space station called *Mir*. By 1987 astronauts were staying on *Mir* for short periods. Important discoveries were being made about how space affects human beings. For the first time in many years, America was behind in the space race.

The Russian space station, *Mir*, was first used in 1987.

THE NEW, IMPROVED SHUTTLE

It cost US $2.4 billion to redesign the shuttle. It looked the same but over 400 changes had been made. Perhaps the most important change was made to the O-rings that sealed parts of the solid rocket motors. NASA called in experts to help with the new design. The O-rings were tested many times. Even so, the ultimate test was taking the shuttle into space.

On 28 September 1988, about 1 million people packed the area around the Kennedy Space Center. In homes up and down the country, millions more people were glued to their television sets. They were all waiting for the launch of space shuttle *Discovery*. It was the first shuttle mission since the *Challenger* disaster. The aim of the mission was to deploy a satellite. But, with so many changes to the design of the shuttle it was also a test flight. Everyone felt nervous. Would the shuttle make it?

The crew of *Discovery* wore new, improved space suits. They were also equipped with an oxygen tank, a parachute, and an inflatable raft.

Discovery launched on
28 September 1988.

As the shuttle cleared the launch pad some people began to cheer. Others held back and waited to hear that the shuttle was safely in orbit. Half an hour after its launch, *Discovery* was 290 kilometres (180 miles) up in space making its first orbit. In the gardens of the White House, President Reagan said, "America is back in space [...] I think I had my fingers crossed like everybody else."

"ALIVE IN OUR HEARTS"

"Today we can say at long last to Dick, Mike, Judy, to Ron and El, and to Christa and Greg, dear friends, we have resumed the journey that we promised to continue for you. Your loss has meant that we can confidently begin anew. Your spirit and your dream are still alive in our hearts."

The crew of STS–26 *Discovery*, the next space shuttle mission to fly after *Challenger*

BACK IN BUSINESS

The space shuttle was back. The following year there were five missions into space. Once more the shuttle was carrying large payloads such as satellites. In 1990 the **Hubble Space Telescope** was launched from *Discovery*. In 1998 the shuttle made its first of many flights to the International Space Station (ISS). Sixteen countries have banded together, including the Russians and Americans, to create this great floating laboratory.

The space shuttle plays an important role in building the ISS as it is used to carry equipment and crew to and from the station.

It was early in the morning of 1 February 2003. *Columbia*, the oldest in NASA's fleet of space shuttles, was about to make its re-entry to Earth. The shuttle had been in space for 16 days. Roughly 16 minutes from landing, *Columbia* tore apart as it re-entered the Earth's atmosphere. Parts of the shuttle were scattered over a huge area, from Texas to Louisiana. There were no survivors. Once more America was in shock. The future of the space shuttle programme was in question again.

TOO OLD TO FLY?

The accident was blamed on a technical failure. During lift-off pieces of debris had hit the left wing of *Columbia*. The flight had probably been doomed from the start. Many people used the examples of the *Challenger* and *Columbia* disasters as reasons to stop the space shuttle programme. They claimed that space travel in the shuttle was too risky and expensive to continue.

Burning debris from *Columbia* was scattered across the sky.

THE SHUTTLE TODAY

"THERE WILL ALWAYS BE A RISK"

"There's a risk in it, and there will always be a risk in it[...] but there's no reason to shut the programme down. It's done too much for humanity. If we did not continue, they would have died in vain."

Grace Corrigan, mother of Christa McAuliffe, commenting after the *Columbia* disaster

"I don't skydive, I don't bungee jump; I don't go on roller coasters, they scare me to death. I'm not that kind of risk taker." These are the words of Colonel Eileen Collins, the commander of *Discovery*. In July 2005 she headed the first space shuttle mission since the *Columbia* disaster of 2003. Although the launch appeared to go according to plan, there were problems. Tiles from the outside of the shuttle broke off and damaged parts of the shuttle.

Everyone was relieved when the shuttle touched down safely on 9 August 2005. NASA still had many questions to answer. It had just spent more than 2 years and US $1 billion trying to improve the design of the shuttle, and problems had still occurred.

The unidentified remains of the crew of *Challenger* were buried at Arlington National Cemetery in Virginia in May 1986.

Clouds over Earth form the background to this picture of *Challenger*.

Many people think the benefits of the space shuttle outweigh the risks. Whatever people choose to believe about the space shuttle programme, they feel terrible sadness at the loss of human life it has led to.

Each year on the anniversary of the *Challenger* disaster, people remember its crew. Some people place flowers near the memorial at Arlington National Cemetery in Virginia, United States. Others visit the Astronaut Memorial at Cape Canaveral. This black, granite wall lists the names of all the astronauts who have died during the US space programme. Many people who visit the memorial feel both a deep sense of pride and a terrible sadness for the crew of *Challenger*.

TIMELINE

1957   The world's first man-made satellite, *Sputnik I*, is put into the Earth's orbit by the Soviet Union. It marks the beginning of the Space Age.

1959   The Soviet Union launches *Luna I*, the first spacecraft to leave Earth's gravity.

1959   The Soviet Union lands the first spacecraft on the Moon, *Luna 2*.

April 1961   The Soviet **cosmonaut** Yuri Gagarin becomes the first person to travel in space.

May 1961   Alan Shepard becomes the first American to travel in space.

1968   The American spacecraft *Apollo 8* becomes the first manned machine to orbit the Moon.

1969   The American astronaut Neil Armstrong becomes the first man to walk on the Moon.

1971   The Soviet Union launches the first space station, *Soviet Salyut I*.

1981   First flight of the space shuttle (*Columbia*).

1982   First commercial satellite is deployed from a space shuttle (*Columbia*).

1983   First spacewalk on a space shuttle mission (*Challenger*).

1983   Astronaut Sally Ride becomes the first American woman in space (*Challenger*).

1983   Astronaut Guion Bluford becomes the first African American in space (*Challenger*).

1983   First Spacelab mission (*Columbia*).

1984   Bruce McCandless makes the first untethered spacewalk from a space shuttle (*Challenger*).

1984   The first satellite is repaired in space (*Challenger*).

1984   Astronaut Kathryn D. Sullivan becomes the first American woman to make a spacewalk (*Challenger*).

28 January 1986	*Challenger* explodes soon after lift-off, killing all seven of the crew.
31 January 1986	Memorial service for the crew of *Challenger* at Johnson Space Center.
3 February 1986	President Ronald Reagan creates a presidential commission to determine the cause of the *Challenger* disaster.
March 1986	The flight deck of *Challenger* is discovered.
9 June 1986	The presidential commission releases its report about the *Challenger* accident.
1986	The Soviets launch the first part of the space station *Mir* into orbit.
28 September 1988	The launch of *Discovery* on the first shuttle mission since the *Challenger* disaster.
1990	Launch of the Hubble Space Telescope (*Discovery*).
1994	The first Russian cosmonaut boards a US space shuttle (*Discovery*).
1995	The first docking of a shuttle with the Russian *Mir* Space Station (*Atlantis*).
1998	The first part of the International Space Station is launched into orbit (*Endeavour*).
2000	NASA celebrates 100 space shuttle missions (*Discovery*)
2003	The space shuttle *Columbia* explodes as it re-enters Earth's atmosphere. All the crew are killed.
2005	Test mission (*Discovery*).

GLOSSARY

appoint choose someone for a job

assassination murder of an important or famous person, such as a president

astronaut person who goes up into space

broadcaster person who makes or sends out television or radio programmes

civilian a person who is not in the armed forces

commander person who is in charge of the crew on a ship or space shuttle

cosmonaut word used by the former Soviet Union to describe a person who goes up into space

crew quarters part of the shuttle where the crew sleeps and eats

debris scattered remains of something

deploy put something in place so it is ready to be used

detonate to set off an explosion

discard throw away or get rid of something

era period in history

flight deck part of the shuttle where the pilot sits and takes control of the flight

flight recorder electronic recording device fitted to an aircraft. A flight recorder can be used to find out the cause of an air crash.

gravity force that pulls things down towards the surface of the Earth and stops them from floating up into space

grounded to be prevented from flying

Halley's Comet comet that travels around the sun leaving a bright trail. It was first recorded in 240 BC.

Hubble Space Telescope telescope that has been in orbit in space since 1990

laboratory room containing special equipment for people to use in scientific experiments

lifeline rope or line attached to an astronaut to stop them from floating into space

maiden voyage first voyage made by a ship or aircraft

memorial service special ceremony held in memory of people or an event

mission journey made for scientific reasons

MMU manned maneuvering unit. A machine like a jet-powered chair that allows astronauts to make untethered spacewalks.

NASA National Aeronautics and Space Administration

news agency organization that collects and distributes news items

orbit path along which something moves around a planet or other body in space

orbiter part of the shuttle designed to fly in orbit

payload a spacecraft's cargo

postpone delay an event

press conference interview given in front of journalists and other members of the press

pressurize keep the air pressure the same as that on the ground

remote-controlled describes machines that can be operated from a distance, usually by radio signals

sacrifice give up something for the sake of another person or thing

satellite machine that can be placed in orbit around Earth. Communication satellites are used to receive and send television and telephone signals.

Soviet Union a union of several areas centred around Russia that existed between 1922 and 1991.

space the universe beyond the edge of Earth's atmosphere

speculate make guesses about the outcome of an event

thrust power created by a jet or rocket engine

T minus phrase used to indicate how many seconds are left before the launch of a space shuttle, e.g. "T minus 10 seconds"

transmit broadcast or show a television or radio programme

untethered not tied to anything

FINDING OUT MORE

BOOKS

Action Books: Fly the Space Shuttle, Carole Stott
(Dorling Kindersley, 1997)

Astronaut: Living in Space, Kate Hayden and Deborah Lock
(Dorling Kindersley, 2000)

Space Travel, Ian Graham (Dorling Kindersley, 2004)

The Amazing Pop-out Pull-out Space Shuttle Pop Up Book,
David Hawcock (Dorling Kindersley, 1998)

The Mammoth Book of Space Exploration and Disasters, Richard
Lawrence (Editor) (Carroll & Graf Publishers, 2005)

The Space Shuttle: A Photographic History, Philip Harrington
(Browntrout, 2003)

THE SHUTTLE ONLINE

spaceflight.nasa.gov
This is the official website of NASA. Find out about the history of
the shuttle programme and read biographies of crew members
and press releases about important events.

www.space.com/shuttlemissions
This site contains information and up-to-date news about the space
shuttle programme. Find out when the next shuttle is expected to
launch, and discover more about space probes and astronomy.

www.heavens-above.com

This website can tell you when it is a good time to see the space station, or any other satellite, from where you live.

www.eduhound.com/columbiatragedy.html

What happened in the *Columbia* disaster? Lots of links and information about the tragedy can be found on this site.

www.seds.org/hst/hst.html

This website contains some of the best images of space taken by the Hubble Space Telescope.

www.solarviews.com//eng/history.htm

Plenty of information about the history of space exploration can be found at this website.

FURTHER RESEARCH

If you are interested in finding out more about space, try researching the following topics:

- space exploration
- Hubble telescope
- astronomers

INDEX